THANK YOU

SET IN SOUL

© 2020 Tatiana Media LLC in partnership with Set In Soul LLC

ISBN #: 978-1-949874-85-3

Published by Tatiana Media LLC

All rights reserved. No part of this journal/publication may be reproduced, stored in a retrieval system, or transmitted in any form or by any means, electronic, mechanical, photocopying, recording, scanning, or otherwise, except as permitted under Section 107 or 108 of the 1976 United States Copyright Act whatsoever without express written permission from the author, except in the case of brief quotations embodied in critical articles and reviews. Please refer all pertinent questions to the publisher.

Limit of Liability/Disclaimer of Warranty: While the publisher and author have used their best efforts in preparing this book/journal, they make no representations or warranties with respect to the accuracy or completeness of the contents of this book/journal and specifically disclaim any implied warranties. The advice and strategies contained herein may not be suitable for your situation. You should consult with a professional where appropriate. Neither the publisher nor author shall be liable for any loss of profit or any other emotional, physical, spiritual and mental distress and damages, including but not limited to special, incidental, consequential, or other damages.

For general information on our other products and services, please contact our Customer Support within the United States at support@setinsoul.com.

Tatiana Media LLC as well as Set In Soul LLC publishes its books in a variety of electronic formats. Some content that appears in print may not be available in electronic books.

THIS JOURNAL BELONGS TO
_____

DEDICATED TO A GIVING
HEART THAT IS NOW
OPEN TO RECEIVING

TABLE OF CONTENTS

How To Use This Journal	6
My Current Receiving Principles	7
Being Able To Receive With Grace	26

HOW TO USE THIS JOURNAL

It's one thing to be a great giver but are you a great receiver? Giving feels good. Giving can make you feel like you are in control. Giving means you are blessed with what you are giving away to something or someone else who may not currently have what you currently possess. Giving produces a happy and healthy spirit when there is trust attached to it. But what about receiving? Are you good at receiving just about anything? Can you receive with grace? Can you receive gifts, compliments, criticism, love, and the tools to help you build what you have asked for? Can you say thank you to whatever it is you are receiving and genuinely mean it?

The pages within this journal are here to help you get to the root of why you may have a hard time receiving certain things. It is within this journal you will start to establish daily practices to help you break down any walls that have been created to stop you from receiving any blessing that requires you to be open. You may have asked over and over again for a particular thing in your life to manifest but because of certain beliefs that no longer serve you in this moment of your life, there is no room for you to receive it. With this journal you will get an idea of how you view others and yourself when it comes to receiving as well as come to a few realizations about yourself that have blocked any ideal situation and solutions from matriculating. You will tear down the walls of pride that is guided by ego and welcome in love and hope into your life. We recommend filling out the prompts in this journal every night to reflect on your day and to set the tone for the next day. The motivational quotes that are sprinkled throughout this journal are there for you to repeat to yourself to release negative thoughts and rebuild new beliefs. There is balance in giving and receiving and we want you to be open enough to genuinely say thank you. Now let's get started.

MY CURRENT RECEIVING PRINCIPLES

MY CURRENT RECEIVING PRINCIPLES

To Me, What Does It Mean To Receive?

I Believe Receivers Are:

I Believe When Someone Gives Something To Me, He/She:

I Do Not Like To Ask For Anything Because (Answer If Applicable):

When Someone Tries To Give Something To Me, I:

MY CURRENT RECEIVING PRINCIPLES

Am I A Good Receiver?

I Expect Others To Receive Anything I Give Them By:

I Believe People Want To Give To Me Because:

I Do Not Like To Accept Anything Because I Believe People Will Think:

I Do Not Like To Accept Anything Because I Believe People Will Find Out:

MY CURRENT RECEIVING PRINCIPLES

Growing Up I Never Received:

Growing Up I Always Received:

When I Use To Ask For Anything, I Always Heard:

I Believe People Give Because:

People Who Receive From Others Are:

MY CURRENT RECEIVING PRINCIPLES

It Is Hard For Me To Take Anything Anyone Gives To Me Because:

Is It Hard For Me To Receive Love (If Yes, Write Down Why)?

Is It Hard For Me To Receive Care (If Yes, Write Down Why)?

Is It Hard For Me To Receive Compliments (If Yes, Write Down Why)?

Receiving An Expensive Gift Makes Me Feel:

MY CURRENT RECEIVING PRINCIPLES

Receiving An Expensive Gift Makes Me Ask:

Receiving A Cheap Gift Makes Me Feel:

Receiving A Cheap Gift Makes Me Ask:

Am I Afraid Of Connection?

Do I Defend/Guard Myself By Not Receiving?

MY CURRENT RECEIVING PRINCIPLES

Does Receiving Anything Make Me Feel Like I Am Surrendering?

If The Answer To The Previous Prompt Is Yes, Why?

Do I Feel Like I Am Being Used When Receiving Gifts Or Compliments?

What Is My Goal In Being Able To Receive Anything?

I Want To Be Able To Receive What?

MY CURRENT RECEIVING PRINCIPLES

Do I Believe It Is Worth Blocking/Stopping What I Stated I Wanted To Receive In The Previous Prompt?

Why Do I Believe My Response To The Previous Prompt?

When I Receive, I Feel The Need:

Things I Have Received In The Past That Have Hurt Me:

Things I Have Received In The Past That Have Made Me Feel Love:

MY CURRENT RECEIVING PRINCIPLES

It Does Not Matter What I Receive, I Will Always:

I Try Not To Receive So I Can Avoid:

Love Comes In These Forms (List Them):

When Someone Tries To Give Me Love Outside Of The Forms I Listed In The Previous Prompt, I Feel:

I Protect My Feelings By:

MY CURRENT RECEIVING PRINCIPLES

I Do Not Know If I Truly Deserve:

My Mother Never Received (Answer If Applicable):

My Mother Could Never Receive (Answer If Applicable):

My Father Never Received (Answer If Applicable):

My Father Could Never Receive (Answer If Applicable):

MY CURRENT RECEIVING PRINCIPLES

When Someone Compliments Me, I Think:

When I Give, I Give Because:

I Was Told When Someone Gives To You:

Everyday I Want To Be Able To:

I Want To Believe:

MY CURRENT RECEIVING PRINCIPLES

I Have A Hard Time Believing:

I Am Worthy Of:

I Know I Need To Let Go Of:

If Everyone Was A Giver And Not A Receiver, Who Would Receive?

I Can Receive And Still Be:

MY CURRENT RECEIVING PRINCIPLES

I Will Break The Misconception That:

I Will No Longer Feel Guilty For:

Why Do I Feel The Way I Feel To My Response To The Previous Prompt?

Who Is The Person Who Wants To Give To Me Right Now?

I Do Not Have To Accept Everything Offered To Me, But I Can Accept:

MY CURRENT RECEIVING PRINCIPLES

When I Do Not Accept Things And Love From People Who Love Me, It Makes Them Feel:

In The Past I Have Chosen Not To Accept Things From Anyone Because:

Recently Someone Who Cared For Me Tried To Give Me:

My Reaction To What Recently Someone Who Cared For Me Tried To Give Me:

Recently Someone I Did Not Know Tried To Give Me:

MY CURRENT RECEIVING PRINCIPLES

My Reaction To What Recently Someone Who I Did Not Know Tried To Give Me:

I Felt (Based On My Response To The Previous Prompt):

Being Self-Sufficient Has Helped Me:

Being Self-Sufficient Has Kept Me From:

When I Receive Criticism, I:

MY CURRENT RECEIVING PRINCIPLES

I Do Not Enjoy Feeling:

What Excuses Do I Make When Someone Wants To Give To Me?

When I Receive Something, I Take Good Care Of It By:

I Can Be Trusted With:

I Believe Compassion Is:

MY CURRENT RECEIVING PRINCIPLES

People Who Support Me:

What Can I Receive From The People Who Support Me?

I Can Receive From The People Who Support Me Because:

What Can I Not Receive From The People That Support Me?

The Reason Why I Cannot Receive What I Listed In The Previous Prompt From People Who Support Me:

MY CURRENT RECEIVING PRINCIPLES

When Receiving Criticism, How Can I Learn Not To Take It Personally?

Do I Value Other People's Opinion?

I Get Defensive When:

Do I Ever Ask For Feedback?

Can I Accept Feedback?

MY CURRENT RECEIVING PRINCIPLES

Can I Accept Help?

Can I Say Thank You?

BEING ABLE TO RECEIVE WITH GRACE

BEING ABLE TO RECEIVE WITH GRACE

Date: Mood:

Today I Received: Today I Rejected The Thought:

I Know I Am Worthy Of: Today I Found Balance In:

Criticism/s I Received Today: I Believe Good Things Are:

I Handled The Criticism/s By: Today's Gifts Are Proof That:

Today I Received Love By: I Allowed _____

                                         To Give Me _____

I Am A Magnet For: Thank You (Write Your Thank You Note For What You Received Whether Favorable Or Not):

BEING ABLE TO RECEIVE WITH GRACE

Date: Mood:

Today I Received: Today I Rejected The Thought:

I Know I Am Worthy Of: Today I Found Balance In:

Criticism/s I Received Today: I Believe Good Things Are:

I Handled The Criticism/s By: Today's Gifts Are Proof That:

Today I Received Love By: I Allowed _____

                                        To Give Me _____

I Am A Magnet For: Thank You (Write Your Thank You
                                        Note For What You Received Whether
                                        Favorable Or Not):

EVERYDAY I AM GETTING BETTER AND BETTER AT RECEIVING AND ACCEPTING.

BEING ABLE TO RECEIVE WITH GRACE

Date: Mood:

Today I Received: Today I Rejected The Thought:

I Know I Am Worthy Of: Today I Found Balance In:

Criticism/s I Received Today: I Believe Good Things Are:

I Handled The Criticism/s By: Today's Gifts Are Proof That:

Today I Received Love By: I Allowed _____

                                         To Give Me _____

I Am A Magnet For: Thank You (Write Your Thank You Note For What You Received Whether Favorable Or Not):

BEING ABLE TO RECEIVE WITH GRACE

Date: Mood:

Today I Received: Today I Rejected The Thought:

I Know I Am Worthy Of: Today I Found Balance In:

Criticism/s I Received Today: I Believe Good Things Are:

I Handled The Criticism/s By: Today's Gifts Are Proof That:

Today I Received Love By: I Allowed _____

                                                   To Give Me _____

I Am A Magnet For: Thank You (Write Your Thank You Note For What You Received Whether Favorable Or Not):

MY PERSONAL THOUGHTS

BEING ABLE TO RECEIVE WITH GRACE

Date: Mood:

Today I Received: Today I Rejected The Thought:

I Know I Am Worthy Of: Today I Found Balance In:

Criticism/s I Received Today: I Believe Good Things Are:

I Handled The Criticism/s By: Today's Gifts Are Proof That:

Today I Received Love By: I Allowed _____

                                           To Give Me _____

I Am A Magnet For: Thank You (Write Your Thank You
                                           Note For What You Received Whether
                                           Favorable Or Not):

I KNOW IT IS OKAY TO SAY YES TO ME.

SOME BIG THINGS I HAVE RECEIVED THAT HAVE CHANGED MY LIFE FOR THE BETTER.....

BEING ABLE TO RECEIVE WITH GRACE

Date: Mood:

Today I Received: Today I Rejected The Thought:

I Know I Am Worthy Of: Today I Found Balance In:

Criticism/s I Received Today: I Believe Good Things Are:

I Handled The Criticism/s By: Today's Gifts Are Proof That:

Today I Received Love By: I Allowed _____

                                         To Give Me _____

I Am A Magnet For: Thank You (Write Your Thank You
                                         Note For What You Received Whether
                                         Favorable Or Not):

BEING ABLE TO RECEIVE WITH GRACE

Date: Mood:

Today I Received: | Today I Rejected The Thought:

I Know I Am Worthy Of: | Today I Found Balance In:

Criticism/s I Received Today: | I Believe Good Things Are:

I Handled The Criticism/s By: | Today's Gifts Are Proof That:

Today I Received Love By: | I Allowed _____

                                                   | To Give Me _____

I Am A Magnet For: | Thank You (Write Your Thank You Note For What You Received Whether Favorable Or Not):

BEING ABLE TO RECEIVE WITH GRACE

Date: Mood:

Today I Received: Today I Rejected The Thought:

I Know I Am Worthy Of: Today I Found Balance In:

Criticism/s I Received Today: I Believe Good Things Are:

I Handled The Criticism/s By: Today's Gifts Are Proof That:

Today I Received Love By: I Allowed _____

                                                  To Give Me _____

I Am A Magnet For: Thank You (Write Your Thank You
                                                  Note For What You Received Whether
                                                  Favorable Or Not):

I STOPPED WORRYING THAT....

BEING ABLE TO RECEIVE WITH GRACE

Date: Mood:

Today I Received: Today I Rejected The Thought:

I Know I Am Worthy Of: Today I Found Balance In:

Criticism/s I Received Today: I Believe Good Things Are:

I Handled The Criticism/s By: Today's Gifts Are Proof That:

Today I Received Love By: I Allowed _____

                                                   To Give Me _____

I Am A Magnet For: Thank You (Write Your Thank You
                                                   Note For What You Received Whether
                                                   Favorable Or Not):

BEING ABLE TO RECEIVE WITH GRACE

Date: Mood:

Today I Received: Today I Rejected The Thought:

I Know I Am Worthy Of: Today I Found Balance In:

Criticism/s I Received Today: I Believe Good Things Are:

I Handled The Criticism/s By: Today's Gifts Are Proof That:

Today I Received Love By: I Allowed _____

                                         To Give Me _____

I Am A Magnet For: Thank You (Write Your Thank You
                                         Note For What You Received Whether
                                         Favorable Or Not):

I DESERVE THAT COMPLIMENT. THANK YOU.

MY PERSONAL THOUGHTS

BEING ABLE TO RECEIVE WITH GRACE

Date: Mood:

Today I Received: Today I Rejected The Thought:

I Know I Am Worthy Of: Today I Found Balance In:

Criticism/s I Received Today: I Believe Good Things Are:

I Handled The Criticism/s By: Today's Gifts Are Proof That:

Today I Received Love By: I Allowed _____

                                           To Give Me _____

I Am A Magnet For: Thank You (Write Your Thank You
                                           Note For What You Received Whether
                                           Favorable Or Not):

BEING ABLE TO RECEIVE WITH GRACE

Date: Mood:

Today I Received: Today I Rejected The Thought:

I Know I Am Worthy Of: Today I Found Balance In:

Criticism/s I Received Today: I Believe Good Things Are:

I Handled The Criticism/s By: Today's Gifts Are Proof That:

Today I Received Love By: I Allowed _____

                                                         To Give Me _____

I Am A Magnet For: Thank You (Write Your Thank You Note For What You Received Whether Favorable Or Not):

I HAVE THE CAPACITY TO RECEIVE THE BEST.

BEING ABLE TO RECEIVE WITH GRACE

Date: Mood:

Today I Received: Today I Rejected The Thought:

I Know I Am Worthy Of: Today I Found Balance In:

Criticism/s I Received Today: I Believe Good Things Are:

I Handled The Criticism/s By: Today's Gifts Are Proof That:

Today I Received Love By: I Allowed _____

                                                   To Give Me _____

I Am A Magnet For: Thank You (Write Your Thank You Note For What You Received Whether Favorable Or Not):

BEING ABLE TO RECEIVE WITH GRACE

Date: Mood:

Today I Received: | Today I Rejected The Thought:

I Know I Am Worthy Of: | Today I Found Balance In:

Criticism/s I Received Today: | I Believe Good Things Are:

I Handled The Criticism/s By: | Today's Gifts Are Proof That:

Today I Received Love By: | I Allowed _____
                                         |
                                         | To Give Me _____

I Am A Magnet For: | Thank You (Write Your Thank You Note For What You Received Whether Favorable Or Not):

BEING ABLE TO RECEIVE WITH GRACE

Date: Mood:

Today I Received: Today I Rejected The Thought:

I Know I Am Worthy Of: Today I Found Balance In:

Criticism/s I Received Today: I Believe Good Things Are:

I Handled The Criticism/s By: Today's Gifts Are Proof That:

Today I Received Love By: I Allowed _____

                                                To Give Me _____

I Am A Magnet For: Thank You (Write Your Thank You Note For What You Received Whether Favorable Or Not):

BEING ABLE TO RECEIVE DOES NOT MAKE ME ANY LESS OF A PERSON.

FIVE THINGS I AM OPEN TO RECEIVING WITHIN THE NEXT SIX MONTHS....

1.

2.

3.

4.

5.

BEING ABLE TO RECEIVE WITH GRACE

Date: Mood:

Today I Received: | Today I Rejected The Thought:

I Know I Am Worthy Of: | Today I Found Balance In:

Criticism/s I Received Today: | I Believe Good Things Are:

I Handled The Criticism/s By: | Today's Gifts Are Proof That:

Today I Received Love By: | I Allowed _____
                                         |
                                         | To Give Me _____

I Am A Magnet For: | Thank You (Write Your Thank You
                                         | Note For What You Received Whether
                                         | Favorable Or Not):

MY PERSONAL THOUGHTS

BEING ABLE TO RECEIVE WITH GRACE

Date: Mood:

Today I Received: Today I Rejected The Thought:

I Know I Am Worthy Of: Today I Found Balance In:

Criticism/s I Received Today: I Believe Good Things Are:

I Handled The Criticism/s By: Today's Gifts Are Proof That:

Today I Received Love By: I Allowed _____

                                         To Give Me _____

I Am A Magnet For: Thank You (Write Your Thank You Note For What You Received Whether Favorable Or Not):

BEING ABLE TO RECEIVE WITH GRACE

Date: Mood:

Today I Received: | Today I Rejected The Thought:

I Know I Am Worthy Of: | Today I Found Balance In:

Criticism/s I Received Today: | I Believe Good Things Are:

I Handled The Criticism/s By: | Today's Gifts Are Proof That:

Today I Received Love By: | I Allowed _____
                                           |
                                           | To Give Me _____

I Am A Magnet For: | Thank You (Write Your Thank You Note For What You Received Whether Favorable Or Not):

BEING ABLE TO RECEIVE WITH GRACE

Date: Mood:

Today I Received: Today I Rejected The Thought:

I Know I Am Worthy Of: Today I Found Balance In:

Criticism/s I Received Today: I Believe Good Things Are:

I Handled The Criticism/s By: Today's Gifts Are Proof That:

Today I Received Love By: I Allowed _____

                                               To Give Me _____

I Am A Magnet For: Thank You (Write Your Thank You Note For What You Received Whether Favorable Or Not):

I AM AN EXCELLENT RECEIVER.

I AM ABLE TO GIVE AND NOW I AM MAKING ROOM TO RECEIVE.

MY PERSONAL THOUGHTS

BEING ABLE TO RECEIVE WITH GRACE

Date: Mood:

Today I Received: Today I Rejected The Thought:

I Know I Am Worthy Of: Today I Found Balance In:

Criticism/s I Received Today: I Believe Good Things Are:

I Handled The Criticism/s By: Today's Gifts Are Proof That:

Today I Received Love By: I Allowed _____

                                         To Give Me _____

I Am A Magnet For: Thank You (Write Your Thank You Note For What You Received Whether Favorable Or Not):

BEING ABLE TO RECEIVE WITH GRACE

Date: Mood:

Today I Received: Today I Rejected The Thought:

I Know I Am Worthy Of: Today I Found Balance In:

Criticism/s I Received Today: I Believe Good Things Are:

I Handled The Criticism/s By: Today's Gifts Are Proof That:

Today I Received Love By: I Allowed _____

                                        To Give Me _____

I Am A Magnet For: Thank You (Write Your Thank You
                                        Note For What You Received Whether
                                        Favorable Or Not):

WHEN I RECEIVE LOVE, IT FEELS....

BEING ABLE TO RECEIVE WITH GRACE

Date: Mood:

Today I Received: | Today I Rejected The Thought:

I Know I Am Worthy Of: | Today I Found Balance In:

Criticism/s I Received Today: | I Believe Good Things Are:

I Handled The Criticism/s By: | Today's Gifts Are Proof That:

Today I Received Love By: | I Allowed _____
                                           |
                                           | To Give Me _____

I Am A Magnet For: | Thank You (Write Your Thank You
                                           | Note For What You Received Whether
                                           | Favorable Or Not):

BEING ABLE TO RECEIVE WITH GRACE

Date: Mood:

Today I Received: | Today I Rejected The Thought:

I Know I Am Worthy Of: | Today I Found Balance In:

Criticism/s I Received Today: | I Believe Good Things Are:

I Handled The Criticism/s By: | Today's Gifts Are Proof That:

Today I Received Love By: | I Allowed _____
                                         |
                                         | To Give Me _____
                                         |
I Am A Magnet For: | Thank You (Write Your Thank You
                                         | Note For What You Received Whether
                                         | Favorable Or Not):

BEING ABLE TO RECEIVE WITH GRACE

Date: Mood:

Today I Received: Today I Rejected The Thought:

I Know I Am Worthy Of: Today I Found Balance In:

Criticism/s I Received Today: I Believe Good Things Are:

I Handled The Criticism/s By: Today's Gifts Are Proof That:

Today I Received Love By: I Allowed _____

                                                         To Give Me _____

I Am A Magnet For: Thank You (Write Your Thank You Note For What You Received Whether Favorable Or Not):

BEING ABLE TO RECEIVE WITH GRACE

Date: Mood:

Today I Received: Today I Rejected The Thought:

I Know I Am Worthy Of: Today I Found Balance In:

Criticism/s I Received Today: I Believe Good Things Are:

I Handled The Criticism/s By: Today's Gifts Are Proof That:

Today I Received Love By: I Allowed _____

                                         To Give Me _____

I Am A Magnet For: Thank You (Write Your Thank You Note For What You Received Whether Favorable Or Not):

I KNOW IT IS OKAY TO SAY I NEED HELP.

JUST BECAUSE I ASK FOR HELP DOES NOT MEAN I AM NOT GOOD ENOUGH.

MY PERSONAL THOUGHTS

BEING ABLE TO RECEIVE WITH GRACE

Date: Mood:

Today I Received: Today I Rejected The Thought:

I Know I Am Worthy Of: Today I Found Balance In:

Criticism/s I Received Today: I Believe Good Things Are:

I Handled The Criticism/s By: Today's Gifts Are Proof That:

Today I Received Love By: I Allowed _____

                                        To Give Me _____

I Am A Magnet For: Thank You (Write Your Thank You Note For What You Received Whether Favorable Or Not):

BEING ABLE TO RECEIVE WITH GRACE

Date: Mood:

Today I Received: Today I Rejected The Thought:

I Know I Am Worthy Of: Today I Found Balance In:

Criticism/s I Received Today: I Believe Good Things Are:

I Handled The Criticism/s By: Today's Gifts Are Proof That:

Today I Received Love By: I Allowed _____

                                         To Give Me _____

I Am A Magnet For: Thank You (Write Your Thank You Note For What You Received Whether Favorable Or Not):

YOU DO NOT HAVE TO BUT THANK YOU.

BEING ABLE TO RECEIVE WITH GRACE

Date: Mood:

Today I Received: | Today I Rejected The Thought:

I Know I Am Worthy Of: | Today I Found Balance In:

Criticism/s I Received Today: | I Believe Good Things Are:

I Handled The Criticism/s By: | Today's Gifts Are Proof That:

Today I Received Love By: | I Allowed _____
                                            |
                                            | To Give Me _____

I Am A Magnet For: | Thank You (Write Your Thank You
                                            | Note For What You Received Whether
                                            | Favorable Or Not):

BEING ABLE TO RECEIVE WITH GRACE

Date: Mood:

Today I Received: Today I Rejected The Thought:

I Know I Am Worthy Of: Today I Found Balance In:

Criticism/s I Received Today: I Believe Good Things Are:

I Handled The Criticism/s By: Today's Gifts Are Proof That:

Today I Received Love By: I Allowed _____

                                                  To Give Me _____

I Am A Magnet For: Thank You (Write Your Thank You Note For What You Received Whether Favorable Or Not):

BEING ABLE TO RECEIVE WITH GRACE

Date: Mood:

Today I Received: Today I Rejected The Thought:

I Know I Am Worthy Of: Today I Found Balance In:

Criticism/s I Received Today: I Believe Good Things Are:

I Handled The Criticism/s By: Today's Gifts Are Proof That:

Today I Received Love By: I Allowed _____

                                                       To Give Me _____

I Am A Magnet For: Thank You (Write Your Thank You Note For What You Received Whether Favorable Or Not):

I AM BLESSED. THAT IS WHY SO MANY THINGS COME TO ME. I AM OPEN TO RECEIVING.

MY PERSONAL THOUGHTS

BEING ABLE TO RECEIVE WITH GRACE

Date: Mood:

Today I Received: Today I Rejected The Thought:

I Know I Am Worthy Of: Today I Found Balance In:

Criticism/s I Received Today: I Believe Good Things Are:

I Handled The Criticism/s By: Today's Gifts Are Proof That:

Today I Received Love By: I Allowed _____

                                         To Give Me _____

I Am A Magnet For: Thank You (Write Your Thank You Note For What You Received Whether Favorable Or Not):

BEING ABLE TO RECEIVE WITH GRACE

Date: Mood:

Today I Received: | Today I Rejected The Thought:

I Know I Am Worthy Of: | Today I Found Balance In:

Criticism/s I Received Today: | I Believe Good Things Are:

I Handled The Criticism/s By: | Today's Gifts Are Proof That:

Today I Received Love By: | I Allowed _____
                                         |
                                         | To Give Me _____

I Am A Magnet For: | Thank You (Write Your Thank You
                                         | Note For What You Received Whether
                                         | Favorable Or Not):

BEING ABLE TO RECEIVE WITH GRACE

Date: Mood:

Today I Received: Today I Rejected The Thought:

I Know I Am Worthy Of: Today I Found Balance In:

Criticism/s I Received Today: I Believe Good Things Are:

I Handled The Criticism/s By: Today's Gifts Are Proof That:

Today I Received Love By: I Allowed _____

                                                   To Give Me _____

I Am A Magnet For: Thank You (Write Your Thank You Note For What You Received Whether Favorable Or Not):

THERE IS GOOD IN RECEIVING. THERE IS GOD IN RECEIVING.

THERE IS NOTHING WRONG WITH BEING A GREAT RECEIVER.

BEING ABLE TO RECEIVE WITH GRACE

Date: Mood:

Today I Received: Today I Rejected The Thought:

I Know I Am Worthy Of: Today I Found Balance In:

Criticism/s I Received Today: I Believe Good Things Are:

I Handled The Criticism/s By: Today's Gifts Are Proof That:

Today I Received Love By: I Allowed _____

                                              To Give Me _____

I Am A Magnet For: Thank You (Write Your Thank You Note For What You Received Whether Favorable Or Not):

BEING ABLE TO RECEIVE WITH GRACE

Date: Mood:

Today I Received: Today I Rejected The Thought:

I Know I Am Worthy Of: Today I Found Balance In:

Criticism/s I Received Today: I Believe Good Things Are:

I Handled The Criticism/s By: Today's Gifts Are Proof That:

Today I Received Love By: I Allowed _____

                                         To Give Me _____

I Am A Magnet For: Thank You (Write Your Thank You Note For What You Received Whether Favorable Or Not):

BEING ABLE TO RECEIVE WITH GRACE

Date: Mood:

Today I Received: Today I Rejected The Thought:

I Know I Am Worthy Of: Today I Found Balance In:

Criticism/s I Received Today: I Believe Good Things Are:

I Handled The Criticism/s By: Today's Gifts Are Proof That:

Today I Received Love By: I Allowed _____

                                                   To Give Me _____

I Am A Magnet For: Thank You (Write Your Thank You Note For What You Received Whether Favorable Or Not):

MY PERSONAL THOUGHTS

RECEIVING WITH APPRECIATION.

BEING ABLE TO RECEIVE WITH GRACE

Date: Mood:

Today I Received: Today I Rejected The Thought:

I Know I Am Worthy Of: Today I Found Balance In:

Criticism/s I Received Today: I Believe Good Things Are:

I Handled The Criticism/s By: Today's Gifts Are Proof That:

Today I Received Love By: I Allowed _____

                                                     To Give Me _____

I Am A Magnet For: Thank You (Write Your Thank You
                                                     Note For What You Received Whether
                                                     Favorable Or Not):

BEING ABLE TO RECEIVE WITH GRACE

Date: Mood:

Today I Received:	Today I Rejected The Thought:
I Know I Am Worthy Of:	Today I Found Balance In:
Criticism/s I Received Today:	I Believe Good Things Are:
I Handled The Criticism/s By:	Today's Gifts Are Proof That:
Today I Received Love By:	I Allowed _____
	To Give Me _____
I Am A Magnet For:	Thank You (Write Your Thank You Note For What You Received Whether Favorable Or Not):

BEING ABLE TO RECEIVE WITH GRACE

Date: Mood:

Today I Received: Today I Rejected The Thought:

I Know I Am Worthy Of: Today I Found Balance In:

Criticism/s I Received Today: I Believe Good Things Are:

I Handled The Criticism/s By: Today's Gifts Are Proof That:

Today I Received Love By: I Allowed _____

                                         To Give Me _____

I Am A Magnet For: Thank You (Write Your Thank You Note For What You Received Whether Favorable Or Not):

WHEN I SEE OTHER PEOPLE RECEIVE THINGS, I THINK.....

BEING ABLE TO RECEIVE WITH GRACE

Date: Mood:

Today I Received: Today I Rejected The Thought:

I Know I Am Worthy Of: Today I Found Balance In:

Criticism/s I Received Today: I Believe Good Things Are:

I Handled The Criticism/s By: Today's Gifts Are Proof That:

Today I Received Love By: I Allowed _____

                                        To Give Me _____

I Am A Magnet For: Thank You (Write Your Thank You Note For What You Received Whether Favorable Or Not):

BEING ABLE TO RECEIVE WITH GRACE

Date: Mood:

Today I Received: Today I Rejected The Thought:

I Know I Am Worthy Of: Today I Found Balance In:

Criticism/s I Received Today: I Believe Good Things Are:

I Handled The Criticism/s By: Today's Gifts Are Proof That:

Today I Received Love By: I Allowed _____

                                         To Give Me _____

I Am A Magnet For: Thank You (Write Your Thank You Note For What You Received Whether Favorable Or Not):

GREAT GIVERS MUST LEARN TO BE GREAT RECEIVERS.

BEING ABLE TO RECEIVE WITH GRACE

Date: Mood:

Today I Received: | Today I Rejected The Thought:

I Know I Am Worthy Of: | Today I Found Balance In:

Criticism/s I Received Today: | I Believe Good Things Are:

I Handled The Criticism/s By: | Today's Gifts Are Proof That:

Today I Received Love By: | I Allowed _____
                                         |
                                         | To Give Me _____

I Am A Magnet For: | Thank You (Write Your Thank You Note For What You Received Whether Favorable Or Not):

BEING ABLE TO RECEIVE WITH GRACE

Date: Mood:

Today I Received: Today I Rejected The Thought:

I Know I Am Worthy Of: Today I Found Balance In:

Criticism/s I Received Today: I Believe Good Things Are:

I Handled The Criticism/s By: Today's Gifts Are Proof That:

Today I Received Love By: I Allowed _____

                                             To Give Me _____

I Am A Magnet For: Thank You (Write Your Thank You Note For What You Received Whether Favorable Or Not):

BEING ABLE TO RECEIVE WITH GRACE

Date: Mood:

Today I Received: | Today I Rejected The Thought:

I Know I Am Worthy Of: | Today I Found Balance In:

Criticism/s I Received Today: | I Believe Good Things Are:

I Handled The Criticism/s By: | Today's Gifts Are Proof That:

Today I Received Love By: | I Allowed _____
                                         |
                                         | To Give Me _____

I Am A Magnet For: | Thank You (Write Your Thank You
                                         | Note For What You Received Whether
                                         | Favorable Or Not):

I MAKE ROOM TO RECEIVE MY BLESSING.

I NO LONGER NEED TO CONTROL....

BEING ABLE TO RECEIVE WITH GRACE

Date: Mood:

Today I Received: Today I Rejected The Thought:

I Know I Am Worthy Of: Today I Found Balance In:

Criticism/s I Received Today: I Believe Good Things Are:

I Handled The Criticism/s By: Today's Gifts Are Proof That:

Today I Received Love By: I Allowed _____

                                         To Give Me _____

I Am A Magnet For: Thank You (Write Your Thank You Note For What You Received Whether Favorable Or Not):

BEING ABLE TO RECEIVE WITH GRACE

Date: Mood:

Today I Received: | Today I Rejected The Thought:

I Know I Am Worthy Of: | Today I Found Balance In:

Criticism/s I Received Today: | I Believe Good Things Are:

I Handled The Criticism/s By: | Today's Gifts Are Proof That:

Today I Received Love By: | I Allowed _____
                                         |
                                         | To Give Me _____

I Am A Magnet For: | Thank You (Write Your Thank You Note For What You Received Whether Favorable Or Not):

SOMETIMES ASKING FOR HELP IS SELF-LOVE.

MY PERSONAL THOUGHTS

BEING ABLE TO RECEIVE WITH GRACE

Date: Mood:

Today I Received: Today I Rejected The Thought:

I Know I Am Worthy Of: Today I Found Balance In:

Criticism/s I Received Today: I Believe Good Things Are:

I Handled The Criticism/s By: Today's Gifts Are Proof That:

Today I Received Love By: I Allowed _____

                                                  To Give Me _____

I Am A Magnet For: Thank You (Write Your Thank You Note For What You Received Whether Favorable Or Not):

WHEN I SET GOALS, I ALWAYS
HOPE TO RECEIVE.....

FROM WHAT/WHO?

BEING ABLE TO RECEIVE WITH GRACE

Date: Mood:

Today I Received: | Today I Rejected The Thought:

I Know I Am Worthy Of: | Today I Found Balance In:

Criticism/s I Received Today: | I Believe Good Things Are:

I Handled The Criticism/s By: | Today's Gifts Are Proof That:

Today I Received Love By: | I Allowed _____
                                        |
                                        | To Give Me _____

I Am A Magnet For: | Thank You (Write Your Thank You
                                        | Note For What You Received Whether
                                        | Favorable Or Not):

BEING ABLE TO RECEIVE WITH GRACE

Date: Mood:

Today I Received: | Today I Rejected The Thought:

I Know I Am Worthy Of: | Today I Found Balance In:

Criticism/s I Received Today: | I Believe Good Things Are:

I Handled The Criticism/s By: | Today's Gifts Are Proof That:

Today I Received Love By: | I Allowed _____
                                           |
                                           | To Give Me _____

I Am A Magnet For: | Thank You (Write Your Thank You Note For What You Received Whether Favorable Or Not):

BEING ABLE TO RECEIVE WITH GRACE

Date: Mood:

Today I Received: | Today I Rejected The Thought:

I Know I Am Worthy Of: | Today I Found Balance In:

Criticism/s I Received Today: | I Believe Good Things Are:

I Handled The Criticism/s By: | Today's Gifts Are Proof That:

Today I Received Love By: | I Allowed _____
                                         |
                                         | To Give Me _____

I Am A Magnet For: | Thank You (Write Your Thank You
                                         | Note For What You Received Whether
                                         | Favorable Or Not):

THE ONLY MISTAKE I MADE WAS NOT ASKING FOR HELP.

BEING ABLE TO RECEIVE WITH GRACE

Date: Mood:

Today I Received: Today I Rejected The Thought:

I Know I Am Worthy Of: Today I Found Balance In:

Criticism/s I Received Today: I Believe Good Things Are:

I Handled The Criticism/s By: Today's Gifts Are Proof That:

Today I Received Love By: I Allowed _____

                                                   To Give Me _____

I Am A Magnet For: Thank You (Write Your Thank You Note For What You Received Whether Favorable Or Not):

BEING ABLE TO RECEIVE WITH GRACE

Date: Mood:

Today I Received: Today I Rejected The Thought:

I Know I Am Worthy Of: Today I Found Balance In:

Criticism/s I Received Today: I Believe Good Things Are:

I Handled The Criticism/s By: Today's Gifts Are Proof That:

Today I Received Love By: I Allowed _____

                                         To Give Me _____

I Am A Magnet For: Thank You (Write Your Thank You Note For What You Received Whether Favorable Or Not):

A RECEIVING HAND IS A BLESSED HAND.

LIST SEVEN GREAT THINGS ABOUT BEING A GREAT RECEIVER.....

1.

2.

3.

4.

5.

6.

7.

BEING ABLE TO RECEIVE WITH GRACE

Date: Mood:

Today I Received: Today I Rejected The Thought:

I Know I Am Worthy Of: Today I Found Balance In:

Criticism/s I Received Today: I Believe Good Things Are:

I Handled The Criticism/s By: Today's Gifts Are Proof That:

Today I Received Love By: I Allowed _____

                                         To Give Me _____

I Am A Magnet For: Thank You (Write Your Thank You Note For What You Received Whether Favorable Or Not):

BEING ABLE TO RECEIVE WITH GRACE

Date: Mood:

Today I Received: Today I Rejected The Thought:

I Know I Am Worthy Of: Today I Found Balance In:

Criticism/s I Received Today: I Believe Good Things Are:

I Handled The Criticism/s By: Today's Gifts Are Proof That:

Today I Received Love By: I Allowed _____

                                         To Give Me _____

I Am A Magnet For: Thank You (Write Your Thank You Note For What You Received Whether Favorable Or Not):

BEING ABLE TO RECEIVE WITH GRACE

Date: Mood:

Today I Received: Today I Rejected The Thought:

I Know I Am Worthy Of: Today I Found Balance In:

Criticism/s I Received Today: I Believe Good Things Are:

I Handled The Criticism/s By: Today's Gifts Are Proof That:

Today I Received Love By: I Allowed _____

                                           To Give Me _____

I Am A Magnet For: Thank You (Write Your Thank You Note For What You Received Whether Favorable Or Not):

I DO NOT HOLD ON TO WHAT I HAVE AS IF THAT IS ALL I HAVE. THAT IS WHY I AM REAPING.

I RECEIVE BECAUSE I ASKED FOR IT.

BEING ABLE TO RECEIVE WITH GRACE

Date: Mood:

Today I Received: | Today I Rejected The Thought:

I Know I Am Worthy Of: | Today I Found Balance In:

Criticism/s I Received Today: | I Believe Good Things Are:

I Handled The Criticism/s By: | Today's Gifts Are Proof That:

Today I Received Love By: | I Allowed _____
                                         |
                                         | To Give Me _____

I Am A Magnet For: | Thank You (Write Your Thank You Note For What You Received Whether Favorable Or Not):

BEING ABLE TO RECEIVE WITH GRACE

Date: Mood:

Today I Received: Today I Rejected The Thought:

I Know I Am Worthy Of: Today I Found Balance In:

Criticism/s I Received Today: I Believe Good Things Are:

I Handled The Criticism/s By: Today's Gifts Are Proof That:

Today I Received Love By: I Allowed _____

                                                    To Give Me _____

I Am A Magnet For: Thank You (Write Your Thank You Note For What You Received Whether Favorable Or Not):

BEING ABLE TO RECEIVE WITH GRACE

Date: Mood:

Today I Received: Today I Rejected The Thought:

I Know I Am Worthy Of: Today I Found Balance In:

Criticism/s I Received Today: I Believe Good Things Are:

I Handled The Criticism/s By: Today's Gifts Are Proof That:

Today I Received Love By: I Allowed _____

                                         To Give Me _____

I Am A Magnet For: Thank You (Write Your Thank You Note For What You Received Whether Favorable Or Not):

IT FEELS GREAT TO....

I AM NOT WEAK JUST BECAUSE I AM BEING BLESSED.

BEING ABLE TO RECEIVE IS ALSO A TRAIT I MUST LEARN.

BEING ABLE TO RECEIVE WITH GRACE

Date: Mood:

Today I Received: Today I Rejected The Thought:

I Know I Am Worthy Of: Today I Found Balance In:

Criticism/s I Received Today: I Believe Good Things Are:

I Handled The Criticism/s By: Today's Gifts Are Proof That:

Today I Received Love By: I Allowed _____

                                               To Give Me _____

I Am A Magnet For: Thank You (Write Your Thank You Note For What You Received Whether Favorable Or Not):

BEING ABLE TO RECEIVE WITH GRACE

Date: Mood:

Today I Received: | Today I Rejected The Thought:
                                         |
                                         |
                                         |
I Know I Am Worthy Of: | Today I Found Balance In:
                                         |
                                         |
                                         |
Criticism/s I Received Today: | I Believe Good Things Are:
                                         |
                                         |
                                         |
I Handled The Criticism/s By: | Today's Gifts Are Proof That:
                                         |
                                         |
                                         |
Today I Received Love By: | I Allowed _____
                                         |
                                         | To Give Me _____
                                         |
I Am A Magnet For: | Thank You (Write Your Thank You
                                         | Note For What You Received Whether
                                         | Favorable Or Not):

BEING ABLE TO RECEIVE WITH GRACE

Date: Mood:

Today I Received: | Today I Rejected The Thought:

I Know I Am Worthy Of: | Today I Found Balance In:

Criticism/s I Received Today: | I Believe Good Things Are:

I Handled The Criticism/s By: | Today's Gifts Are Proof That:

Today I Received Love By: | I Allowed _____
                                         |
                                         | To Give Me _____

I Am A Magnet For: | Thank You (Write Your Thank You
                                         | Note For What You Received Whether
                                         | Favorable Or Not):

IT IS OKAY TO ACCEPT THIS GIFT.

BEING ABLE TO RECEIVE WITH GRACE

Date: Mood:

Today I Received: | Today I Rejected The Thought:

I Know I Am Worthy Of: | Today I Found Balance In:

Criticism/s I Received Today: | I Believe Good Things Are:

I Handled The Criticism/s By: | Today's Gifts Are Proof That:

Today I Received Love By: | I Allowed _____
                                         |
                                         | To Give Me _____

I Am A Magnet For: | Thank You (Write Your Thank You Note For What You Received Whether Favorable Or Not):

BEING ABLE TO RECEIVE WITH GRACE

Date: Mood:

Today I Received: Today I Rejected The Thought:

I Know I Am Worthy Of: Today I Found Balance In:

Criticism/s I Received Today: I Believe Good Things Are:

I Handled The Criticism/s By: Today's Gifts Are Proof That:

Today I Received Love By: I Allowed _____

                                        To Give Me _____

I Am A Magnet For: Thank You (Write Your Thank You
                                        Note For What You Received Whether
                                        Favorable Or Not):

IT IS OKAY TO BE ACKNOWLEDGED FOR MY WORK.

I AM ABLE TO SAY THANK YOU.

BEING ABLE TO RECEIVE WITH GRACE

Date: Mood:

Today I Received: Today I Rejected The Thought:

I Know I Am Worthy Of: Today I Found Balance In:

Criticism/s I Received Today: I Believe Good Things Are:

I Handled The Criticism/s By: Today's Gifts Are Proof That:

Today I Received Love By: I Allowed _____

                                                  To Give Me _____

I Am A Magnet For: Thank You (Write Your Thank You Note For What You Received Whether Favorable Or Not):

BEING ABLE TO RECEIVE WITH GRACE

Date: Mood:

Today I Received: | Today I Rejected The Thought:
                                   |
                                   |
I Know I Am Worthy Of: | Today I Found Balance In:
                                   |
                                   |
Criticism/s I Received Today: | I Believe Good Things Are:
                                   |
                                   |
I Handled The Criticism/s By: | Today's Gifts Are Proof That:
                                   |
                                   |
Today I Received Love By: | I Allowed _____
                                   |
                                   | To Give Me _____
                                   |
I Am A Magnet For: | Thank You (Write Your Thank You
                                   | Note For What You Received Whether
                                   | Favorable Or Not):

RECEIVING CREATES CONNECTION AND I WILL NO LONGER FEAR CONNECTING.

BEING ABLE TO RECEIVE WITH GRACE

Date: Mood:

Today I Received: Today I Rejected The Thought:

I Know I Am Worthy Of: Today I Found Balance In:

Criticism/s I Received Today: I Believe Good Things Are:

I Handled The Criticism/s By: Today's Gifts Are Proof That:

Today I Received Love By: I Allowed _____

                                         To Give Me _____

I Am A Magnet For: Thank You (Write Your Thank You Note For What You Received Whether Favorable Or Not):

BEING ABLE TO RECEIVE WITH GRACE

Date: Mood:

Today I Received: Today I Rejected The Thought:

I Know I Am Worthy Of: Today I Found Balance In:

Criticism/s I Received Today: I Believe Good Things Are:

I Handled The Criticism/s By: Today's Gifts Are Proof That:

Today I Received Love By: I Allowed _____

                                         To Give Me _____

I Am A Magnet For: Thank You (Write Your Thank You Note For What You Received Whether Favorable Or Not):

I NO LONGER LONGER DO IT ON MY OWN.

MY PERSONAL THOUGHTS

BEING ABLE TO RECEIVE WITH GRACE

Date: Mood:

Today I Received: | Today I Rejected The Thought:

I Know I Am Worthy Of: | Today I Found Balance In:

Criticism/s I Received Today: | I Believe Good Things Are:

I Handled The Criticism/s By: | Today's Gifts Are Proof That:

Today I Received Love By: | I Allowed _____
                                           |
                                           | To Give Me _____

I Am A Magnet For: | Thank You (Write Your Thank You
                                           | Note For What You Received Whether
                                           | Favorable Or Not):

BEING ABLE TO RECEIVE WITH GRACE

Date: Mood:

Today I Received: Today I Rejected The Thought:

I Know I Am Worthy Of: Today I Found Balance In:

Criticism/s I Received Today: I Believe Good Things Are:

I Handled The Criticism/s By: Today's Gifts Are Proof That:

Today I Received Love By: I Allowed _____

                                         To Give Me _____

I Am A Magnet For: Thank You (Write Your Thank You
                                         Note For What You Received Whether
                                         Favorable Or Not):

I CAN ACCEPT HELP AND STILL HAVE EVERYTHING TOGETHER.

BEING A BETTER RECEIVER IS MAKING ME A BETTER....

BEING ABLE TO RECEIVE WITH GRACE

Date: Mood:

Today I Received: Today I Rejected The Thought:

I Know I Am Worthy Of: Today I Found Balance In:

Criticism/s I Received Today: I Believe Good Things Are:

I Handled The Criticism/s By: Today's Gifts Are Proof That:

Today I Received Love By: I Allowed _____

                                                   To Give Me _____

I Am A Magnet For: Thank You (Write Your Thank You Note For What You Received Whether Favorable Or Not):

BEING ABLE TO RECEIVE WITH GRACE

Date: Mood:

Today I Received: Today I Rejected The Thought:

I Know I Am Worthy Of: Today I Found Balance In:

Criticism/s I Received Today: I Believe Good Things Are:

I Handled The Criticism/s By: Today's Gifts Are Proof That:

Today I Received Love By: I Allowed _____

                                           To Give Me _____

I Am A Magnet For: Thank You (Write Your Thank You Note For What You Received Whether Favorable Or Not):

BEING ABLE TO RECEIVE WITH GRACE

Date: Mood:

Today I Received: | Today I Rejected The Thought:

I Know I Am Worthy Of: | Today I Found Balance In:

Criticism/s I Received Today: | I Believe Good Things Are:

I Handled The Criticism/s By: | Today's Gifts Are Proof That:

Today I Received Love By: | I Allowed _____
                                         |
                                         | To Give Me _____

I Am A Magnet For: | Thank You (Write Your Thank You
                                         | Note For What You Received Whether
                                         | Favorable Or Not):

I LOVE MY SUPPORT SYSTEM.

IT IS OKAY FOR ME TO ALLOW OTHERS TO SUPPORT ME IN MY ENDEAVORS.

BEING ABLE TO RECEIVE WITH GRACE

Date: Mood:

Today I Received: | Today I Rejected The Thought:

I Know I Am Worthy Of: | Today I Found Balance In:

Criticism/s I Received Today: | I Believe Good Things Are:

I Handled The Criticism/s By: | Today's Gifts Are Proof That:

Today I Received Love By: | I Allowed _____
                                         |
                                         | To Give Me _____

I Am A Magnet For: | Thank You (Write Your Thank You
                                         | Note For What You Received Whether
                                         | Favorable Or Not):

BEING ABLE TO RECEIVE WITH GRACE

Date: Mood:

Today I Received: Today I Rejected The Thought:

I Know I Am Worthy Of: Today I Found Balance In:

Criticism/s I Received Today: I Believe Good Things Are:

I Handled The Criticism/s By: Today's Gifts Are Proof That:

Today I Received Love By: I Allowed _____

                                    To Give Me _____

I Am A Magnet For: Thank You (Write Your Thank You Note For What You Received Whether Favorable Or Not):

MY PERSONAL THOUGHTS

BEING ABLE TO RECEIVE WITH GRACE

Date: Mood:

Today I Received: Today I Rejected The Thought:

I Know I Am Worthy Of: Today I Found Balance In:

Criticism/s I Received Today: I Believe Good Things Are:

I Handled The Criticism/s By: Today's Gifts Are Proof That:

Today I Received Love By: I Allowed _____

                                               To Give Me _____

I Am A Magnet For: Thank You (Write Your Thank You Note For What You Received Whether Favorable Or Not):

BEING ABLE TO RECEIVE WITH GRACE

Date: Mood:

Today I Received: Today I Rejected The Thought:

I Know I Am Worthy Of: Today I Found Balance In:

Criticism/s I Received Today: I Believe Good Things Are:

I Handled The Criticism/s By: Today's Gifts Are Proof That:

Today I Received Love By: I Allowed _____

                                         To Give Me _____

I Am A Magnet For: Thank You (Write Your Thank You
                                         Note For What You Received Whether
                                         Favorable Or Not):

I WILL ALLOW YOU TO LOVE ME.

PEOPLE AROUND ME WHO WANT ME TO BE A BETTER RECEIVER....

BEING ABLE TO RECEIVE WITH GRACE

Date: Mood:

Today I Received: Today I Rejected The Thought:

I Know I Am Worthy Of: Today I Found Balance In:

Criticism/s I Received Today: I Believe Good Things Are:

I Handled The Criticism/s By: Today's Gifts Are Proof That:

Today I Received Love By: I Allowed _____

                                         To Give Me _____

I Am A Magnet For: Thank You (Write Your Thank You Note For What You Received Whether Favorable Or Not):

BEING ABLE TO RECEIVE WITH GRACE

Date: Mood:

Today I Received: | Today I Rejected The Thought:

I Know I Am Worthy Of: | Today I Found Balance In:

Criticism/s I Received Today: | I Believe Good Things Are:

I Handled The Criticism/s By: | Today's Gifts Are Proof That:

Today I Received Love By: | I Allowed _____
                                         |
                                         | To Give Me _____

I Am A Magnet For: | Thank You (Write Your Thank You
                                         | Note For What You Received Whether
                                         | Favorable Or Not):

I SET MY PRIDE ASIDE.

MY EGO WILL NOT DICTATE WHAT I WILL SAY YES OR NO TO.

BEING VULNERABLE TO ME MEANS.....

MY PERSONAL THOUGHTS

BEING ABLE TO RECEIVE WITH GRACE

Date: Mood:

Today I Received: Today I Rejected The Thought:

I Know I Am Worthy Of: Today I Found Balance In:

Criticism/s I Received Today: I Believe Good Things Are:

I Handled The Criticism/s By: Today's Gifts Are Proof That:

Today I Received Love By: I Allowed _____

                                         To Give Me _____

I Am A Magnet For: Thank You (Write Your Thank You
                                         Note For What You Received Whether
                                         Favorable Or Not):

BEING ABLE TO RECEIVE WITH GRACE

Date: Mood:

Today I Received: Today I Rejected The Thought:

I Know I Am Worthy Of: Today I Found Balance In:

Criticism/s I Received Today: I Believe Good Things Are:

I Handled The Criticism/s By: Today's Gifts Are Proof That:

Today I Received Love By: I Allowed _____

                                                           To Give Me _____

I Am A Magnet For: Thank You (Write Your Thank You
                                                           Note For What You Received Whether
                                                           Favorable Or Not):

BEING ABLE TO RECEIVE WITH GRACE

Date: Mood:

Today I Received: | Today I Rejected The Thought:
                                         |
                                         |
I Know I Am Worthy Of: | Today I Found Balance In:
                                         |
                                         |
Criticism/s I Received Today: | I Believe Good Things Are:
                                         |
                                         |
I Handled The Criticism/s By: | Today's Gifts Are Proof That:
                                         |
                                         |
Today I Received Love By: | I Allowed _____
                                         |
                                         | To Give Me _____
                                         |
I Am A Magnet For: | Thank You (Write Your Thank You Note For What You Received Whether Favorable Or Not):

BEING ABLE TO RECEIVE WITH GRACE

Date: Mood:

Today I Received: | Today I Rejected The Thought:

I Know I Am Worthy Of: | Today I Found Balance In:

Criticism/s I Received Today: | I Believe Good Things Are:

I Handled The Criticism/s By: | Today's Gifts Are Proof That:

Today I Received Love By: | I Allowed _____
                                           |
                                           | To Give Me _____

I Am A Magnet For: | Thank You (Write Your Thank You Note For What You Received Whether Favorable Or Not):

IT
FEELS
GOOD
TO BE
LOVED.

BEING ABLE TO RECEIVE WITH GRACE

Date: Mood:

Today I Received: | Today I Rejected The Thought:

I Know I Am Worthy Of: | Today I Found Balance In:

Criticism/s I Received Today: | I Believe Good Things Are:

I Handled The Criticism/s By: | Today's Gifts Are Proof That:

Today I Received Love By: | I Allowed _____
                                         |
                                         | To Give Me _____

I Am A Magnet For: | Thank You (Write Your Thank You
                                         | Note For What You Received Whether
                                         | Favorable Or Not):

BEING ABLE TO RECEIVE WITH GRACE

Date: Mood:

Today I Received: Today I Rejected The Thought:

I Know I Am Worthy Of: Today I Found Balance In:

Criticism/s I Received Today: I Believe Good Things Are:

I Handled The Criticism/s By: Today's Gifts Are Proof That:

Today I Received Love By: I Allowed _____

                                               To Give Me _____

I Am A Magnet For: Thank You (Write Your Thank You
                                               Note For What You Received Whether
                                               Favorable Or Not):

I AM NOT HELPLESS, I AM WISE. I KNOW WHEN TO ASK FOR HELP.

BEING ABLE TO RECEIVE WITH GRACE

Date: Mood:

Today I Received: Today I Rejected The Thought:

I Know I Am Worthy Of: Today I Found Balance In:

Criticism/s I Received Today: I Believe Good Things Are:

I Handled The Criticism/s By: Today's Gifts Are Proof That:

Today I Received Love By: I Allowed _____

                                         To Give Me _____

I Am A Magnet For: Thank You (Write Your Thank You
                                         Note For What You Received Whether
                                         Favorable Or Not):

BEING ABLE TO RECEIVE WITH GRACE

Date: Mood:

Today I Received: Today I Rejected The Thought:

I Know I Am Worthy Of: Today I Found Balance In:

Criticism/s I Received Today: I Believe Good Things Are:

I Handled The Criticism/s By: Today's Gifts Are Proof That:

Today I Received Love By: I Allowed _____

                                         To Give Me _____

I Am A Magnet For: Thank You (Write Your Thank You Note For What You Received Whether Favorable Or Not):

BEING ABLE TO RECEIVE WITH GRACE

Date: Mood:

Today I Received: Today I Rejected The Thought:

I Know I Am Worthy Of: Today I Found Balance In:

Criticism/s I Received Today: I Believe Good Things Are:

I Handled The Criticism/s By: Today's Gifts Are Proof That:

Today I Received Love By: I Allowed _____

                                                To Give Me _____

I Am A Magnet For: Thank You (Write Your Thank You Note For What You Received Whether Favorable Or Not):

I AM NOT AFRAID TO BE VULNERABLE.

I AM GETTING BETTER AT RECEIVING LOVE.

BEING ABLE TO RECEIVE WITH GRACE

Date: Mood:

Today I Received: Today I Rejected The Thought:

I Know I Am Worthy Of: Today I Found Balance In:

Criticism/s I Received Today: I Believe Good Things Are:

I Handled The Criticism/s By: Today's Gifts Are Proof That:

Today I Received Love By: I Allowed _____

                                                  To Give Me _____

I Am A Magnet For: Thank You (Write Your Thank You Note For What You Received Whether Favorable Or Not):

BEING ABLE TO RECEIVE WITH GRACE

Date: Mood:

Today I Received: | Today I Rejected The Thought:

I Know I Am Worthy Of: | Today I Found Balance In:

Criticism/s I Received Today: | I Believe Good Things Are:

I Handled The Criticism/s By: | Today's Gifts Are Proof That:

Today I Received Love By: | I Allowed _____
                                         |
                                         | To Give Me _____

I Am A Magnet For: | Thank You (Write Your Thank You
                                         | Note For What You Received Whether
                                         | Favorable Or Not):

BEING ABLE TO RECEIVE WITH GRACE

Date: Mood:

Today I Received: Today I Rejected The Thought:

I Know I Am Worthy Of: Today I Found Balance In:

Criticism/s I Received Today: I Believe Good Things Are:

I Handled The Criticism/s By: Today's Gifts Are Proof That:

Today I Received Love By: I Allowed _____

                                         To Give Me _____

I Am A Magnet For: Thank You (Write Your Thank You Note For What You Received Whether Favorable Or Not):

MY PRIDE....

BEING ABLE TO RECEIVE WITH GRACE

Date: Mood:

Today I Received: | Today I Rejected The Thought:

I Know I Am Worthy Of: | Today I Found Balance In:

Criticism/s I Received Today: | I Believe Good Things Are:

I Handled The Criticism/s By: | Today's Gifts Are Proof That:

Today I Received Love By: | I Allowed _____
                                         |
                                         | To Give Me _____

I Am A Magnet For: | Thank You (Write Your Thank You Note For What You Received Whether Favorable Or Not):

BEING ABLE TO RECEIVE WITH GRACE

Date: Mood:

Today I Received: | Today I Rejected The Thought:

I Know I Am Worthy Of: | Today I Found Balance In:

Criticism/s I Received Today: | I Believe Good Things Are:

I Handled The Criticism/s By: | Today's Gifts Are Proof That:

Today I Received Love By: | I Allowed _____
                                         |
                                         | To Give Me _____

I Am A Magnet For: | Thank You (Write Your Thank You
                                         | Note For What You Received Whether
                                         | Favorable Or Not):

BEING ABLE TO RECEIVE WITH GRACE

Date: Mood:

Today I Received: Today I Rejected The Thought:

I Know I Am Worthy Of: Today I Found Balance In:

Criticism/s I Received Today: I Believe Good Things Are:

I Handled The Criticism/s By: Today's Gifts Are Proof That:

Today I Received Love By: I Allowed _____

                                         To Give Me _____

I Am A Magnet For: Thank You (Write Your Thank You Note For What You Received Whether Favorable Or Not):

I AM SAYING YES TO LOVE.

BEING ABLE TO RECEIVE WITH GRACE

Date: Mood:

Today I Received: Today I Rejected The Thought:

I Know I Am Worthy Of: Today I Found Balance In:

Criticism/s I Received Today: I Believe Good Things Are:

I Handled The Criticism/s By: Today's Gifts Are Proof That:

Today I Received Love By: I Allowed _____

                                              To Give Me _____

I Am A Magnet For: Thank You (Write Your Thank You Note For What You Received Whether Favorable Or Not):

BEING ABLE TO RECEIVE WITH GRACE

Date: Mood:

Today I Received: Today I Rejected The Thought:

I Know I Am Worthy Of: Today I Found Balance In:

Criticism/s I Received Today: I Believe Good Things Are:

I Handled The Criticism/s By: Today's Gifts Are Proof That:

Today I Received Love By: I Allowed _____

                                         To Give Me _____

I Am A Magnet For: Thank You (Write Your Thank You
                                         Note For What You Received Whether
                                         Favorable Or Not):

BEING ABLE TO RECEIVE WITH GRACE

Date: Mood:

Today I Received: Today I Rejected The Thought:

I Know I Am Worthy Of: Today I Found Balance In:

Criticism/s I Received Today: I Believe Good Things Are:

I Handled The Criticism/s By: Today's Gifts Are Proof That:

Today I Received Love By: I Allowed _____

                                         To Give Me _____

I Am A Magnet For: Thank You (Write Your Thank You
                                         Note For What You Received Whether
                                         Favorable Or Not):

MY PERSONAL THOUGHTS

FIVE WAYS I CAN PLEASANTLY RECEIVE CRITICISM....

1.

2.

3.

4.

5.

BEING ABLE TO RECEIVE WITH GRACE

Date: Mood:

Today I Received: Today I Rejected The Thought:

I Know I Am Worthy Of: Today I Found Balance In:

Criticism/s I Received Today: I Believe Good Things Are:

I Handled The Criticism/s By: Today's Gifts Are Proof That:

Today I Received Love By: I Allowed _____

                                         To Give Me _____

I Am A Magnet For: Thank You (Write Your Thank You
                                         Note For What You Received Whether
                                         Favorable Or Not):

BEING ABLE TO RECEIVE WITH GRACE

Date: Mood:

Today I Received: | Today I Rejected The Thought:

I Know I Am Worthy Of: | Today I Found Balance In:

Criticism/s I Received Today: | I Believe Good Things Are:

I Handled The Criticism/s By: | Today's Gifts Are Proof That:

Today I Received Love By: | I Allowed _____

                                       | To Give Me _____

I Am A Magnet For: | Thank You (Write Your Thank You Note For What You Received Whether Favorable Or Not):

BEING ABLE TO RECEIVE WITH GRACE

Date: Mood:

Today I Received: Today I Rejected The Thought:

I Know I Am Worthy Of: Today I Found Balance In:

Criticism/s I Received Today: I Believe Good Things Are:

I Handled The Criticism/s By: Today's Gifts Are Proof That:

Today I Received Love By: I Allowed _____

                                         To Give Me _____

I Am A Magnet For: Thank You (Write Your Thank You
                                         Note For What You Received Whether
                                         Favorable Or Not):

DISAPPOINTMENT WILL NOT STOP ME FROM HAVING A RECEIVING HEART.

I AM SAYING YES. I AM SAYING YES.

BEING ABLE TO RECEIVE WITH GRACE

Date: Mood:

Today I Received: Today I Rejected The Thought:

I Know I Am Worthy Of: Today I Found Balance In:

Criticism/s I Received Today: I Believe Good Things Are:

I Handled The Criticism/s By: Today's Gifts Are Proof That:

Today I Received Love By: I Allowed _____

                                                    To Give Me _____

I Am A Magnet For: Thank You (Write Your Thank You Note For What You Received Whether Favorable Or Not):

BEING ABLE TO RECEIVE WITH GRACE

Date: Mood:

Today I Received: | Today I Rejected The Thought:

I Know I Am Worthy Of: | Today I Found Balance In:

Criticism/s I Received Today: | I Believe Good Things Are:

I Handled The Criticism/s By: | Today's Gifts Are Proof That:

Today I Received Love By: | I Allowed _____
                                         |
                                         | To Give Me _____

I Am A Magnet For: | Thank You (Write Your Thank You Note For What You Received Whether Favorable Or Not):

I AM WORTHY OF A HELPING HAND.

BEING ABLE TO RECEIVE WITH GRACE

Date: Mood:

Today I Received: Today I Rejected The Thought:

I Know I Am Worthy Of: Today I Found Balance In:

Criticism/s I Received Today: I Believe Good Things Are:

I Handled The Criticism/s By: Today's Gifts Are Proof That:

Today I Received Love By: I Allowed _____

                                         To Give Me _____

I Am A Magnet For: Thank You (Write Your Thank You Note For What You Received Whether Favorable Or Not):

BEING ABLE TO RECEIVE WITH GRACE

Date: Mood:

Today I Received: Today I Rejected The Thought:

I Know I Am Worthy Of: Today I Found Balance In:

Criticism/s I Received Today: I Believe Good Things Are:

I Handled The Criticism/s By: Today's Gifts Are Proof That:

Today I Received Love By: I Allowed _____

                                                   To Give Me _____

I Am A Magnet For: Thank You (Write Your Thank You Note For What You Received Whether Favorable Or Not):

BEING ABLE TO RECEIVE WITH GRACE

Date: Mood:

Today I Received: Today I Rejected The Thought:

I Know I Am Worthy Of: Today I Found Balance In:

Criticism/s I Received Today: I Believe Good Things Are:

I Handled The Criticism/s By: Today's Gifts Are Proof That:

Today I Received Love By: I Allowed _____

                                         To Give Me _____

I Am A Magnet For: Thank You (Write Your Thank You Note For What You Received Whether Favorable Or Not):

BEING ABLE TO RECEIVE WITH GRACE

Date: Mood:

Today I Received: | Today I Rejected The Thought:

I Know I Am Worthy Of: | Today I Found Balance In:

Criticism/s I Received Today: | I Believe Good Things Are:

I Handled The Criticism/s By: | Today's Gifts Are Proof That:

Today I Received Love By: | I Allowed _____
                                                      |
                                                      | To Give Me _____

I Am A Magnet For: | Thank You (Write Your Thank You
                                                      | Note For What You Received Whether
                                                      | Favorable Or Not):

199

MY PERSONAL THOUGHTS

I MAY NOT LIKE TO DEPEND ON PEOPLE BUT I LOVE TO DEPEND ON GOD WHO SENDS PEOPLE MY WAY TO HELP ME.

RECEIVING DOES NOT MAKE ME WEAK.

BEING ABLE TO RECEIVE WITH GRACE

Date: Mood:

Today I Received: Today I Rejected The Thought:

I Know I Am Worthy Of: Today I Found Balance In:

Criticism/s I Received Today: I Believe Good Things Are:

I Handled The Criticism/s By: Today's Gifts Are Proof That:

Today I Received Love By: I Allowed _____

                                         To Give Me _____

I Am A Magnet For: Thank You (Write Your Thank You
                                         Note For What You Received Whether
                                         Favorable Or Not):

BEING ABLE TO RECEIVE WITH GRACE

Date: Mood:

Today I Received: Today I Rejected The Thought:

I Know I Am Worthy Of: Today I Found Balance In:

Criticism/s I Received Today: I Believe Good Things Are:

I Handled The Criticism/s By: Today's Gifts Are Proof That:

Today I Received Love By: I Allowed _____

                                         To Give Me _____

I Am A Magnet For: Thank You (Write Your Thank You
                                         Note For What You Received Whether
                                         Favorable Or Not):

BEING ABLE TO RECEIVE WITH GRACE

Date: Mood:

Today I Received: Today I Rejected The Thought:

I Know I Am Worthy Of: Today I Found Balance In:

Criticism/s I Received Today: I Believe Good Things Are:

I Handled The Criticism/s By: Today's Gifts Are Proof That:

Today I Received Love By: I Allowed _____

                                                    To Give Me _____

I Am A Magnet For: Thank You (Write Your Thank You
                                                    Note For What You Received Whether
                                                    Favorable Or Not):

I CAN ACCEPT A COMPLIMENT GRACIOUSLY.

BEING ABLE TO RECEIVE WITH GRACE

Date: Mood:

Today I Received: Today I Rejected The Thought:

I Know I Am Worthy Of: Today I Found Balance In:

Criticism/s I Received Today: I Believe Good Things Are:

I Handled The Criticism/s By: Today's Gifts Are Proof That:

Today I Received Love By: I Allowed _____

                                                  To Give Me _____

I Am A Magnet For: Thank You (Write Your Thank You Note For What You Received Whether Favorable Or Not):

BEING ABLE TO RECEIVE WITH GRACE

Date: Mood:

Today I Received: Today I Rejected The Thought:

I Know I Am Worthy Of: Today I Found Balance In:

Criticism/s I Received Today: I Believe Good Things Are:

I Handled The Criticism/s By: Today's Gifts Are Proof That:

Today I Received Love By: I Allowed _____

                                         To Give Me _____

I Am A Magnet For: Thank You (Write Your Thank You Note For What You Received Whether Favorable Or Not):

BEING ABLE TO RECEIVE WITH GRACE

Date: Mood:

Today I Received: Today I Rejected The Thought:

I Know I Am Worthy Of: Today I Found Balance In:

Criticism/s I Received Today: I Believe Good Things Are:

I Handled The Criticism/s By: Today's Gifts Are Proof That:

Today I Received Love By: I Allowed _____

                                                   To Give Me _____

I Am A Magnet For: Thank You (Write Your Thank You
                                                   Note For What You Received Whether
                                                   Favorable Or Not):

MY PERSONAL THOUGHTS

THERE IS NO SPECIAL REWARD FOR DOING IT ALL BY YOURSELF.

I DESERVE PEACE.

BEING ABLE TO RECEIVE WITH GRACE

Date: Mood:

Today I Received: Today I Rejected The Thought:

I Know I Am Worthy Of: Today I Found Balance In:

Criticism/s I Received Today: I Believe Good Things Are:

I Handled The Criticism/s By: Today's Gifts Are Proof That:

Today I Received Love By: I Allowed _____

                                                   To Give Me _____

I Am A Magnet For: Thank You (Write Your Thank You
                                                   Note For What You Received Whether
                                                   Favorable Or Not):

BEING ABLE TO RECEIVE WITH GRACE

Date: Mood:

Today I Received: | Today I Rejected The Thought:

I Know I Am Worthy Of: | Today I Found Balance In:

Criticism/s I Received Today: | I Believe Good Things Are:

I Handled The Criticism/s By: | Today's Gifts Are Proof That:

Today I Received Love By: | I Allowed _____
                                         |
                                         | To Give Me _____

I Am A Magnet For: | Thank You (Write Your Thank You
                                         | Note For What You Received Whether
                                         | Favorable Or Not):

BEING ABLE TO RECEIVE WITH GRACE

Date: Mood:

Today I Received: Today I Rejected The Thought:

I Know I Am Worthy Of: Today I Found Balance In:

Criticism/s I Received Today: I Believe Good Things Are:

I Handled The Criticism/s By: Today's Gifts Are Proof That:

Today I Received Love By: I Allowed _____

                                                  To Give Me _____

I Am A Magnet For: Thank You (Write Your Thank You Note For What You Received Whether Favorable Or Not):

MY PERSONAL THOUGHTS

BEING ABLE TO RECEIVE WITH GRACE

Date: Mood:

Today I Received: Today I Rejected The Thought:

I Know I Am Worthy Of: Today I Found Balance In:

Criticism/s I Received Today: I Believe Good Things Are:

I Handled The Criticism/s By: Today's Gifts Are Proof That:

Today I Received Love By: I Allowed _____

                                                  To Give Me _____

I Am A Magnet For: Thank You (Write Your Thank You
                                                  Note For What You Received Whether
                                                  Favorable Or Not):

BEING ABLE TO RECEIVE WITH GRACE

Date: Mood:

Today I Received: Today I Rejected The Thought:

I Know I Am Worthy Of: Today I Found Balance In:

Criticism/s I Received Today: I Believe Good Things Are:

I Handled The Criticism/s By: Today's Gifts Are Proof That:

Today I Received Love By: I Allowed _____

                                                   To Give Me _____

I Am A Magnet For: Thank You (Write Your Thank You Note For What You Received Whether Favorable Or Not):

BEING ABLE TO RECEIVE WITH GRACE

Date: Mood:

Today I Received: | Today I Rejected The Thought:

I Know I Am Worthy Of: | Today I Found Balance In:

Criticism/s I Received Today: | I Believe Good Things Are:

I Handled The Criticism/s By: | Today's Gifts Are Proof That:

Today I Received Love By: | I Allowed _____
                                               |
                                               | To Give Me _____

I Am A Magnet For: | Thank You (Write Your Thank You
                                               | Note For What You Received Whether
                                               | Favorable Or Not):

BEING ABLE TO RECEIVE WITH GRACE

Date: Mood:

Today I Received: Today I Rejected The Thought:

I Know I Am Worthy Of: Today I Found Balance In:

Criticism/s I Received Today: I Believe Good Things Are:

I Handled The Criticism/s By: Today's Gifts Are Proof That:

Today I Received Love By: I Allowed _____

                                         To Give Me _____

I Am A Magnet For: Thank You (Write Your Thank You Note For What You Received Whether Favorable Or Not):

SOME THINGS ARE BIGGER THAN ME SO IT REQUIRES MORE THAN JUST ME.

STRENGTHENING MY ABILITY TO SAY YES.

BEING ABLE TO RECEIVE WITH GRACE

Date: Mood:

Today I Received: Today I Rejected The Thought:

I Know I Am Worthy Of: Today I Found Balance In:

Criticism/s I Received Today: I Believe Good Things Are:

I Handled The Criticism/s By: Today's Gifts Are Proof That:

Today I Received Love By: I Allowed _____

                                                   To Give Me _____

I Am A Magnet For: Thank You (Write Your Thank You
                                                   Note For What You Received Whether
                                                   Favorable Or Not):

BEING ABLE TO RECEIVE WITH GRACE

Date: Mood:

Today I Received: Today I Rejected The Thought:

I Know I Am Worthy Of: Today I Found Balance In:

Criticism/s I Received Today: I Believe Good Things Are:

I Handled The Criticism/s By: Today's Gifts Are Proof That:

Today I Received Love By: I Allowed _____

                                               To Give Me _____

I Am A Magnet For: Thank You (Write Your Thank You
                                               Note For What You Received Whether
                                               Favorable Or Not):

BEING ABLE TO RECEIVE WITH GRACE

Date: Mood:

Today I Received: | Today I Rejected The Thought:

I Know I Am Worthy Of: | Today I Found Balance In:

Criticism/s I Received Today: | I Believe Good Things Are:

I Handled The Criticism/s By: | Today's Gifts Are Proof That:

Today I Received Love By: | I Allowed _____

To Give Me _____

I Am A Magnet For: | Thank You (Write Your Thank You Note For What You Received Whether Favorable Or Not):

STRONG PEOPLE ARE GREAT RECEIVERS.

Made in the USA
Middletown, DE
17 March 2020